D1558798

Mulled Psalms

Mulled Psalms

∽ Moving from I to We ∽

MARJORIE GRAY

RESOURCE *Publications* · Eugene, Oregon

MULLED PSALMS
Moving from I to We

Resource Publications
An Imprint of Wipf and Stock Publishers
199 W. 8th Ave., Suite 3
Eugene, OR 97401

www.wipfandstock.com

ISBN 13: 978-1-4982-0439-2

Manufactured in the U.S.A.   05/12/2016

～ Introduction

What better way to satisfy spiritual thirst than with the Psalms' rich brew? Mulling or reflecting on Holy Spirit-breathed Scripture, we can "be filled with the Spirit, speaking to one another with psalms, hymns, and songs from the Spirit" (Eph 5:18–19). Like all poems, the psalms are meant for mulling. Like all Scripture, they are meant for day and night meditation. This savoring begins in the far reaches of our unique psyches at the mysterious, musical borderlines of heart and mind. It continues as, alone or together, we imbibe the potent, spirited brew, reading slowly, audibly, and breathing deeply between the lines. Like divine love and creativity, the delights of psalm-mulling always grow, never end.

God always surges as the strongest current in Psalms' mullstream. The indescribable Great Spirit is the one with whom we most long to converse. Could this be because God longs even more to reveal Godself as Love in order to commune with us? It's not surprising that God as Jesus is alive in Psalms. He told two of his early followers: "Everything must be fulfilled that is written about me in the Law of Moses, the Prophets and the Psalms" (Luke 24:44).

Mulling opens our heart eyes to see God as Loving Creator, and humankind as God's good children, throughout the psalm-stream. Nature's marvels awe humans today no less than ancient people, hopefully more, due to scientific discoveries. But most hours of most days we're blinded by self-absorption; our spiritual taste buds are deadened by competition. Psalms of lament or complaint with temptations of revenge resonate in every decade as the almighty dollar mandates violence against people, land, water and air. What relief to realize God's re-creative reach, however hidden, in every psalm! What encouragement for those working and praying for God's rule "on earth as in heaven"!

INTRODUCTION

Welcome now, dear readers and listeners, to this outpouring of psalm poems. May you be gently nudged, as I am constantly, from frenzied, false self to God-imaging true being; from ego and empire building to heart, mind, soul worship; from isolation and conflict to family and community. May each mulled psalm inspire new mulling, as well as refreshing tastes of the original psalms and all of Scripture.

~ 1

Happy ones ignore talking heads;
Glad souls repel liars,
never befriend jabbing jokers.
Rather they savor Live Words at all hours:
like river-irrigated forests God-
freshened, Joyous Peace-seekers thrive.
What of God-denouncers?
Hapless dust-balls, self-made justifiers—
hopeless, ruthless, they are devoid of trust.
God Who sees all knows who is Just.
Violence blinds and self-destructs.

~ 2

World leaders, why presume? How dare
figureheads flaunt selves, tout isms,
defying the Transcendent One?
Listen, posturing technocrats!
Holy Love laughs sadly. Listen!
Shiver under God's displeasure.
Hear God name Creation's Ruler,
empowering Peace Prince to topple
regimes and pulverize shackles.
Kings, presidents, come and kneel now.
Love and serve with Servant Master,
always radiant, always at Peace.

~ 3

God! Hundreds of adversaries!
Thousands versus only me…us?

Holy Fire, Divine Protector:
keep me shining; buoy our spirits.

From Your wide, high, unbiased View
we trust You will answer our cries.

Every night I sleep serenely;
each new dawn brings Your renewing.

Stalwart angel warriors dispel
worry, dread, every doom carrier.

Holy Master of Tenderness,
free us from cycling avengers.

Void their careless, spiteful lashes;
make them bite their own word bullets.

God, You are our Liberator:
keep us Joyful, ever Peaceful.

～ 4

God? God, can I get a reply?
See me boxed in, calling, calling.

When will You end people's mocking,
smoking pipe-dreams, fetish worship?

God, You called us to Your service;
Loving one, we know You hear us.

Now in awe I let go anger,
probe my motives, wait in silence.

People strive for fame, for money;
let Your Smile be my fulfillment.

Joy from You exceeds all measures;
rest is safe, serene my slumber.

≈ 5

Unseen one, hear me crying "Help!"
God, can You understand my sobs?

Every morning You receive us,
offering up ourselves in worship,
hopeful, eager for Your Spirit.

Surly people gain no access
but humble love impels approach;
we kneel awestruck in joyous praise.

Guide us, Spirit, past attackers;
all their words reek with hatred.
God, please cause their schemes to backfire.

Let those who know You gladly sing;
under Your Assault-proof Cover
may Your loving ones enjoy You.

Life with You is Carefree, Wondrous!
We're Refreshed, Embraced, Protected.

~ 6

Holy One, please do not scold
or treat us harshly.
God, I am exhausted:
heal her aching body;
lift his beaten spirit.
Will Your Love revive us?
How? When? Must we die first?
Sleepless, always weeping,
tired of grieving, we are
sick to death of fights.

Back off, demons! God is Listening,
Receiving each tear, prayer and sigh.
All antagonists, retreat and,
mortified, lay down your weapons.

~ 7

God Alive, our Hideout: Strong Love,
rescue us from haters' talons.
If we have betrayed our families
or even have loathed enemies,
our defeat may be well-deserved.
God, overcome our blind anger
by Your Calm, Straightforward Judgment.
Rise, preside, and vindicate us:
Wise One, You see our true motives.
Halt all violent endeavors;
guard each truthful, peaceful spirit.
Your Passionate Justice awes us.
Mischief plotters hatch mere bubbles;
trouble-makers drown in trouble.

Thank You, Proactive Advocate;
All praise to You, God Majestic.

~ 8

Your Excellency! Cosmos Creator,
Celestial King: babies sound Your praises;
children's chanting shames Your foes to silence.

God Whose fingers flung out planets and spun
myriad galaxies into orbit:
Do mere humans merit Your attention?
Do You honor us almost as angels?

You adorn our lives with Glorious Purpose
to tend life on land, in air and water.
God, Your Majesty! Holy Creator!

~ 9

With heart-driven poems we long to praise You.
Celebrating Your astounding actions
we rejoice in Your majestic presence.
May our songs trumpet Your supreme honor.
Accusers give up their case against us,
stunned to face You, Defender of Justice.

Divine One, do You devastate nations
and decimate vengeful, vicious people?
All-Viewing One, You always judge justly,
shelter outcasts, safeguard troubled masses.
God, to know You is to trust You, the One
Who never turns from those who look for You.

You remember and punish bloodshed,
never overlook mistreated people.
God, look on us today in Your Mercy;
draw us from the panicked brink of despair.
May we freely publicize Your Kindness,
thriving in Your Ever-Living power.

Let God-denying regimes self-destruct,
lost in labyrinths designed to trap others.
Your Justice is famous. Wily leaders
who forget You die and are forgotten.
You never forget one needy person
but offer Hope to each soul that suffers.

∾ 10

Why the seeming chasm between us?
God, can You see how much we need You?
Prideful hustlers prey on poor families:
they flaunt obscene lifestyles, kiss up to
landlords, warlords; they curse You, despise
your law. Fat-cats brag "Nothing scares us."
Bigwigs talk big, pile on threats and lies.
Cronies bully women, hurt children:
safety nets are severed while dragnets
keep ensnaring innocent weaklings.
Sneaky thieves assume You are blind, God.

Heaven, hear and rescue beaten ones.
Why permit perpetrators' curses
with boasts that You will never judge them?
All-Seeing One, You see the suffering!
Weigh each groan and teardrop, for victims
depend on You. Break evildoers'
power; call them to account. Divine
Judge, You rule the Universe in Peace:
violent empires have no future.
Loving God, You draw close to those who
yearn for shelter, water, food, freedom.
You move us to care, to encourage,
to advocate for abandoned ones.
No more fear of humans or demons.

~ 11

We are safe here with You, God.
Why this fearful urge to flee?
We see danger and evil
spiraling—bombs, hijackings,
crumbling buildings—what to do?

You preside in Holy Splendor
shining through all Creation's facets.
You observe every person closely,
prove our intentions sullied or pure.

You will brand violent people;
fiery guilt pangs will consume them,
Great Spirit will sweep them away.

God, You are good. You love justice.
You will guide us to face Your love.

~ 12

God, help! No one is faithful.
Humans cannot be trusted;
everyone's words are empty—
bloated untruths, glazed with sweet talk.

God, please seal flattering mouths.
Mute minds that boast "We always
win with words—who can stymie us?"

Messiah, keep the promises:
You hear needy people's groans;
You will stop thieves of poor folks.

Your Words gleam like sun on ice,
Pure as baby's first teardrops.

Love, safeguard hassled people;
extricate us from rat-racers
who parade degradation.

~ 13

Mercy, God, how much longer?
When, if ever, will we see You?
When will global conflict end?
How long will horrors persist?

Do You realize our confusion?
Let us see You; help us know You.
Otherwise we sink and drown while
gloaters smile to see us flounder.

But we trust Your loving power;
your provision keeps us joyful,
overflowing with new love songs.
Thank You, divine ever-close Friend.

～ 14

Foolish hearts insist there is no God.
Rotten characters rape and bribe;
no one is good. God is looking:

is anyone looking for God?
Does anybody understand?
No, all are headstrong; none do right.

Arrogant critics, can't You see?
You are swallowing up people
and thereby disrespecting God!

Dread will overwhelm You because
Holy Advocate stands with victims.
Though crooks bulldoze poor people's dreams

God's live word resurrects vision,
spurs actions toward Earth's Renewal!
Let the festive singing begin.

～ 15

Great Spirit, who is welcome in Your
Secret Place? Who is at home there?

Those with bright, clean lifestyles, sincere
folks who do not backbite or revile.

These humble, brave souls cannot be
swayed by vileness or violence.
They affirm all who respect God.

No matter the consequences, they
keep their word. The poor can borrow
interest-free—no penalties, no bribes.

What a beautiful, solid life!

~ 16

Spirit, hover close:
keep us under cover, Master.
Our work is worthless
without Your Leading.

Hooray for Godly People,
Friends of Earth, our True Friends always.
Idol fan-club crazies
will capsize weekly, daily.
We refuse them tribute,
not gracing their names with mention.

Love Source God, our Benefactor:
thanks for jobs that provide plenty.
Praise to You, Loving Spirit
Whose Counsel lights our night musings.

Keep us focused, Holy Guide,
purpose clear, in sync with You.
Joy will buoy our hearty voicing;
Your Sweet Peace eases all strained nerves.

Breath of all Creation's Life,
breathe through us Your Re-creation.
Life-Way Escort, thank You;
we are Alive in Love always.

～ 17

Grant us a hearing, God:
our plea is warranted;
we're telling the whole truth.
Pronounce us not guilty.
You see our true motives;
You probe our heart mind links
for night-hatched plots, and find
no deceit, greed or spite.
Because we follow You,
money or violence
cannot seduce us.
When we pray we know You
listen and will answer.
Reveal Your Wondrous Love
to harassed refugees.
Watch us like a Mother;
shelter and protect us
from those whose words can kill.
Threat-hurlers surround us:
their proud mouths yip and yap;
from hard-shelled hearts clammed shut
their mean looks pummel us.
Face them down now, Spirit.
Free us from high-flying
doom-deservers who stuff
their bored children senseless.

We will see You and rest
our case in the morning.

~ 18

God, we love You, we trust Your power;
Spirit, You're our Sanctuary Tower.
When we called, Huge Holy Love,
You rescued us from every gun.

Deadness slithered across our spirits
spewing venom without limits.
Cornered, we cried "Help!" O God, You heard;
Heaven's Tender Ear bent earthward.

Tremors rattled rocks, shook mountains;
holy anger spurted molten.
You split skies, ripped through storm clouds,
crackled light beams and spattered ice drops.

You voiced rage in flood and thunder
but did not leave us floundering.
Holy Spirit, You held us close,
transported us to Your Safe House.

Far from rip-off gangs and hecklers we played;
You sang us lullabies, kept us loyal.
Faithful people know You faithful;
healthy ones in You are healthful.

Truthful speakers find Your Word true,
but deceivers refuse to face You.
God, Your Grace promotes the humble
and causes proud ones to stumble.

Your Brilliance fires our courage,
dazzles foes and burns all blockage.
Your Life-Way is perfect in wisdom,
Your protection boulder solid.

Who else can claim to be divine?
On whom but You can we rely?
Ready, set to deter conflict
we deflect darts by Your Spirit.

You expunge our dread of failure,
gently bolstering our endurance.
Hail, Ever-Living Ruler of all:
Your Love ignites worldwide awe.

～ 19

Galaxies shine with Your genius;
skies unveil Your masterpieces—
ever singing day-song, night-song,
soundless telling, ceaseless, boundless.
Love, You stretched our sun's blue canvas;
there Your virile dawn light dances,
warming all by Earth's revolving.

Scripture's truth, like nature's order
steadies every reeling spirit.
God, Your Laws make sense for humans
on the way to joyful wisdom;
Your decrees persist in brilliance,
awesome, true for all forever;
Your Great Book stands timeless, tireless—
valued, savored beyond compare.

Priceless warning signs of peril,
Your commands reward obeyers.
Who can see their own wrongs, Father?
God, forgive our blind indifference;
steer us clear of stubborn fault-lines,
free to thrive on Your Pilgrim Way,
guiltless, guileless in Your Presence.
May our musings please Your Honor—
Holy Lifeguard, God our anchor.

∿ 20

Mr. President, we pray God
answers you, relieves your stress load,
keeps you with family in green zone.

May your help be always Godsent,
honest work by joyful people.

Hearts of rulers looking heavenward,
your best desires will be fulfilled.

Leaders, giving Love the credit,
we rejoice at your elections.

May God hear your daily prayers,
affirm your winsome words and ways.

Many put their trust in weapons;
may Peace be your core reliance.

Fighters falter, but Love keeps us
firmly grounded.

          Hear us, Master:
crown Your servant leaders' efforts.

∼ 21

Leaders, leap for joy with Spirit energy!
God fulfills your longings, faithful rulers, freely
grants requests you offer. King Divine will honor
justice-working governors, give you livelong success.

Spirit, You infuse us with Joy;
Your Strong Love will hold us steady.
(When will destroyers be destroyed,
and odious deeds nullified?)

Hail, God of all! Highest accolades!

∿ 22

God, why have You left me alone?
Why Your distance from her bleeding,
silence to his all-night pleading?

Holy Supreme Benefactor,
trusted God of our grandparents:
You heard and helped our ancestors
but we're helpless. Sneering mockers
jab and slash our Scripture Worldview;
yet from birth You have embraced us.

Be here now as terror threatens;
bullies bash her prospects senseless,
they string him up, parched, stripped, tortured
God, where are You? Please be near;
You're our Invisible Defense.
Breathe our bones alive, God Spirit.

We believe You suffer with us;
God, we vow to praise You always,
worship You and serve Your poor ones.
Keep us listening, praying, thriving.
Global is Your Peaceful Kingdom:
every people group will know You;
poor and rich will kneel before You;
every child will hear Your Story—
Stunning Truth, Astounding Glory.

～ 23

Divine Guardian, You care for us;
You provide all we need, and more,
taking us to serene, green places
where we are refreshed to the core.

You show us Right Ways,
trails Your Ranger blazed.
Not even death's gloom traumatizes us
on the path to Your Lighthouse.

We are safe and strong:
with so-called enemies
You invite us to feast, carefree,
blessed with effervescent health.

Your passionate compassion
always invigorates us;
we'll be Down Home forever
with You, Joyful Peacemaker.

~ 24

Our planet belongs to You:
all that lives gets Life from You
Who made this Wonderful Place;
You brought Order from chaos,
called forth myriad species.
Who dares approach Your Summit?
Who can face Your Holiness?

The forgiven ones and those
who give others a clean slate.
They are not swayed by money,
not lured by fame or bias.
You smile on them; Your Peace
shines through them for all to see.
They're the God-looking people.

Look up, rulers! Heads up, public servants!
Make way for the Preeminent One.
Who is preeminent?
The Courageous Servant Leader
Who faces down violence
and deactivates death.

Look, rulers! Listen, administrators!
Make way for the Most Brilliant One.
Who is most brilliant?
The Crown Prince of World Peace,
the Majestic Creator.

~ 25

Royal guide, with You I walk tall.
Keep me confident in You,
never disgraced by challengers
or traumatized by criminals.

Teach me, Wonder-Wise Counselor;
all my life I need Your Guidance.
God, recall Your Kindness to me;
please forget my youthful misdeeds.

You guide blind fools, addicts, all
who humbly admit being lost.
You walk us along New Life Paths
and erase our regretful records.

Who kneels in prayer? Your students.
We will be healthy Earth-Keepers,
awestruck discoverers of secrets,
realizers of Promises Come True.

Spirit of God, we need You now—
I need You inside me, beside us—
hurt, stressed, grieving, agonizing.
Lift the burdens of our failures.

You are the Gateway to Peace Place.
Keep us walking tall, Royal Guide;
our Confidence is still in You.
Rescue all tormented children.

～ 26

God, pronounce me guilt-free:
You know my pure longings;
see me through Your Love Eyes;
look into my heart, read my mind.

God, we know that You
Love us and we love You.
Liars, pretenders and
wrong-doers we avoid.
God, we want to come clean,
come to celebrate You,
go all out in worship.

What joy to walk with You
seeing Your Creation!
Let me not be enticed
by anger, hate or greed.

You know our pure desires;
we trust Your Divine Love.
With You we're on firm ground
singing altogether.

～ 27

My Life-Light, my Energy,
my Healing Power is God.
No one can frighten us now.
Fear-mongers threaten and bluff
but tumble from their own thrones.
Though thousands enlist for war
we will not give in to terror.

God, all I ask You is this:
to stay in Your Home-Free Place,
enthralled by Holy Brilliance,
exploring Wisdom's terrain.
You will shelter us always;
grounded deep, heads and hopes high,
our praises will ever rise.

Holy Spirit, hear my call:
heart to heart I long for God.
Are You aloof or distant?
You've always been our Guardian;
please don't give up on us now.
You will welcome us, even
if family and friends do not.

Trailblazer, show us Your Way;
let no demon have a say.
We perceive Your New Reign's dawn;
over all Your Love will shine.
We await You with courage!

~ 28

Hello? Are You there, God?
Can You hear me? Are You listening?
Help! Eyes of God, see us crying,
straining toward Your Holy Presence

while old combatants drag us down.
May they drink their own poison brew
(just deserts for deserting You).
Dismiss them permanently, God.

Hello! Thank You for listening!
You are my Cover and Vigor.
We dance and sing in childlike joy;
I leap into Your Trusty Arms.

Vibrant vicar of Your People,
Kind Parent, Divine Bodyguard:
Revive Your Family; bring every
lost heir home in Glad Reunion.

∾ 29

Worship Lovejoy King, all beings of light,
angel processions in blinding brilliance.

Worship King of Peace, transparent people;
reflect Divine Radiance. Hear Creator

boom in ocean waves, roar in cataracts:
"Magnificent! Omnipotent!"

Listen, awestruck: hear cedar trees crack,
grand boulders rumble, reel with seismic quakes.
Watch lightning zip-zap.

From forest floor littered with fallen limbs
to swaying crowns of towering oaks
all Creation's chorus resounds in awe.

Peace-Giver presides, quelling all chaos,
empowering Earth-Keepers.

～ 30

God, we love praising You
Who raised us from despair,
silencing rivals' glee.
When we shouted "God, help!"
You restored us, drew us
out of deadly sinkholes.

Worship God with joyous music
all you loving, loyal people.
Love's anger is rare and fleeting;
compassion holds strong forever.
Night-time sobbing? Sunrise smiles!

O God, we took You for granted,
bragged that we would never stumble.
No surprise we felt abandoned,
whimpering "O God we're dying,
who will voice kudos in graveyards?"

You Transformed us: no more bawling;
now we laugh, dance, sing every day,
bursting with glad creative praise!

～ 31

God, we seek asylum!
Mute the scorn; bring justice, freedom!
Where can we live? How survive?
Gentle Shepherd, guide our steps
away from landmines to Your Homeland.
We entrust our lives to You
with abandon, fleeing idol fan clubs.
We're carefree with You, Spirit, Who discerned
our pressing cares, brought us out from under.
But millions struggle, trapped in crises.
Crying eyes of victims haunt us;
we groan for malnourished children
mired in grief with anguished parents.
Callous leaders stir up terror
squashing hopes and killing peace dreams.
Friends and family follow blindly,
shun our pleas as broken records.
But You, God of Peace, we count on:
You will handle every time bomb,
foil the hands that grab and cuff us.
Shame each heartless rogue with failure;
silence liars; let despisers die soon.
In Your Presence we are hidden
safe from dog-eat-dog confusion.
All praise to You, Divine Lover!
When besieged we couldn't see You
but You heard our desperate pleading.
Be encouraged, sisters, brothers;
keep hope high, True Promise trusters.

～ 32

God, Your forgiven ones are merry,
honest, guilt-free in Your Wide Mercy.

Trying to hide or deny sins,
my energy died beneath Your frown
but when I faced up, came clean,
what relief You gave! Forgave all.

Let every wannabe do-gooder
pray to You, Loving Listening One.
You will wall off inundating floods.

Holy Presence, secret protection:
Your Embrace deflects raucous chaos,
fills our minds with rescue music.

"I'll be your Teacher" You tell us.
"I'll watch and guide you with Tender Care;
don't react with knee-jerk rebellion."

Devilish players pile up sorrows
but True Love signs multiply
all around Your trusting followers.

People with God-honoring desires:
sing out wild grateful joy!

~ 33

Sing for joy to God, straight-talkers;
praise is natural for life-lovers.
Strum jazz guitars, ripple keyboards;
write great hymns, create new music
for the Voice of Sacred Scripture's
Master Author ever rings true.

God Who prizes Truth and Justice
fills the world with nature's Love Notes.
By Divine Wisdom's ordering
stars emerged, galaxies were born,
lands arose from wild waters.
Attention! Stand in awe of God
Whose Voice creates and activates.

God confounds warlords' strategies;
Divine Peace Plans cannot be foiled.
God-loving groups thrive in Glad Lands.
God our Maker sees our actions.
Mega-armies can't keep us safe;
brute force, breakneck speed lead nowhere.

Spirit shines through Love-Way pilgrims,
takes us through drought and death to Life.
We wait, relying on our Guide,
full of Joy. God, keep us near You.

～ 34

Twenty-four seven we yearn to praise,
whisper "Yes, Love" with each waking breath,
yearn to show hurting people God is Good,
yearn to come together singing hoorays.

I looked for someone when I was scared stiff;
an angel banished my paralysis,
carried me beyond every trouble
to where light surrounds God-worshipers.

Savor Divine Love, everyone;
revere God in holy simplicity.
Hunger weakens strong young hunters
but God-searchers are fully satisfied.
Love living? Yearn for a long, good life?
Watch your words, nothing foul or false;
avoid violence; follow Peace Path blazes.

God's Kind Eyes and Ears hold humble humans
but brutes will be deleted from all screens.
God responds to honest soul cries,
comes close when hearts fracture,
restores life to knocked out spirits.

We all make or step in messes
but God brings us out in one piece.
Culprits' own sick lifestyles kill them;
Divine Counselor's rehab frees us.

~ 35

Attack the attackers, God.
Suit us with Hate-Proof Armor,
wielding Your Word Baton.
Holy Spirit, be our Secret Service;
blow away life-draining demons.
Some try lacing truth with nonsense:
catch them with their own catch phrases;
shock them by their own short circuits.

I shout from my truest self:
"God, You are the Greatest!—
Champion of the helpless poor."
Fast talkers fire questions,
hurl barbs into peace talks.
Those we have cared for like family
smile at our misery.
God, why the centuries long delay?
Come, rescue us from fear's clutches;
we long to praise You in great crowds.

God, stop blind, proud haters; stop those
mockers of humble Earth-Tenders;
shame those who kick people around.
Let justice-doers' joy erupt in song,
honoring You Who enjoy
filling Your servants' lives with joy.
God, may all our voices laud You always.

～ 36

God, hear blind self-admirers'
snide laughter, piled on strident
in-your-face, godless chatter.
Read their minds at midnight, processing spite.

Holy God of endless, sky-high, True Love:
Your Justice is ocean-wide;
You Care for all who are alive;
we Flourish in nature's intricate web.

God, how exquisite Your Love!
You calm our panicked spirits,
nourishing us with Wisdom.
Enjoying You we discover New Joys.

Source of all Love: keep our love bold and true,
playing, singing New Heart Tunes.
Let no snobbish mind pervade;
may self-worshipers trip up, slip away.

～ 37

We tell each other:
Stop stewing about happy-go-lucky
fiends; they will shrivel like scorched grass.
Bank on God; do good work; enjoy Earth's gifts;
love God and be free of want.
See God's Spirit brightening all we do
like sunbeams at dawn and noon.
Hold still for God, jumpy minds:
listen; wait; breathe in God's Spirit.
Stop stewing over wealthy scoundrels;
anger cooks our own goose, boils off goodness.

To God's humble dependents
Earth is bequeathed in Peaceful Abundance
after greedy crooks abscond.
Wars displace and maim poor friends;
ruthless leaders destroy good citizens;
their bombs kill their own children.
God's Love Power trumps coercion.

Though God-fighters flash, they will fizzle,
drowned in debt—while God-lovers keep giving—
joyous, vibrant and healthy.
Elders say they have never seen
kind people lonely or their kids hungry.
Watch people who do good deeds:
there is a bright future for Peacemakers—
in the trenches, then Home Free with God.

~ 38

Divine Parent, please don't lash out at Your
hurting children, wounded by Your anger,
beaten down under Your frown,
infested with guilt.

One hates herself for foolish binges;
deep in debt, she never stops weeping.
Another is old and listless
with a sore back killing him.

O God, we long to help ease their pain:
we sigh with her; his hurts crease our faces;
our hearts break for many more.
Our vision decays.

People avoid us, sick of our grieving
while landmines explode under children's feet.
Strategists ignore dire needs;
officials deceive.

We turn inward, tongue-tied, waiting for You—
God, we trust You: please show us what to do.
May we not bow to tycoons
who boast of their loot.

Wise Judge, we admit our wrongs and failures
but we are despised for being poor.
Holy Spirit, help us endure;
keep our motives pure.

~ 39

Told each other: Talk
will only aggravate.
Resolved: No words when
opponents are around.

Quiet for many days,
no voice pro or con.
But emotions boiled,
could not stay silent.

God, is my life over?
Help me confront death.
Life is a mere moment
no matter poor or rich.

God, what's our future?
You alone bring hope:
free us from sin's grip;
silence senseless scorners.

Told each other: Be still—
God is in control.
But we can't bear this
austere discipline.

God, listen, help us please:
help all refugees.
Help me find Your Peace
with Joy before I die.

～ 40

We were patients in God's waiting room:
wretched and weeping we waited until
Someone heard us crying, drew us from gloom
to gladness, murky swamp to lofty hill.

Spirit infuses us with New Praise Poems
(may they rouse others with awe for God).
People who trust God will enjoy Shalom,
immune to all the hype of demigods.

God plans and acts in countless wondrous ways.
Words fail us: God, You're incomparable!
You ask nothing for us to do or say
yet through us You make Yourself palpable.

We hear and see ourselves in Your Story.
Hearts united, we yearn to follow You:
we pray our work will bring You honor, God;
we bare our souls to show Your Love is True.

Keep us near You, Holy One: protect us
from harms others do or we do ourselves.
We are inundated, losing focus
in blame-and-shame mazes again. God, help!

～ 41

God Blesses people who
care about poor people;
God Rescues and Shelters,
Heals and Blesses people.

Father, forgive and restore us:
our tangles have broken Love's Bonds.
Haters presume we are goners;
friends and family turn against us.

Yet Your Forgiveness restores us,
preserving our integrity.
Keep us always in Your Pure Love.
All praise to God then, now, always!

∿ 42

Like dehydrated children
we thirst for You, Life-Giving God.
When can we drink our fill of Your Spirit?
All we can taste is the salt of our tears.
People keep jeering "Where is God?"
while the marrow of our lives runs out.
We used to love gathering to worship You;
full of Your Spirit, we loved singing hymns.
"What's the problem?" we ask each other:
"Why these doldrums?"
We need to zero in on You, God,
voicing Your praise again, Liberator.
Morose, withdrawn, we recall Your Splendor
from lush valley to mountain peaks.
Our churning emotions reverberate
with waterfalls and ocean waves.
All day You pour forth Love, Lifespring Fountain;
at night we dream up prayer poems
to You, our Deep Thirst Quencher.
Spirit of God, Eternal Mountain Spring:
"Why do we feel You don't care anymore?
Why are we always weeping,
weighed down by life-sappers
who keep taunting 'Where is God now?'"
"What's the problem?" we ask each other:
"Why these doldrums?"
We need to zero in on You, God,
voicing Your praise again, Liberator.

~ 43

Justify Your followers, God:
defend us against false charges
contrived by heartless cheaters.

We know You are our Champion.
Why do we feel abandoned?
Why are we always grieving,
weighed down by life-sappers?

Beam Your Brilliance on us,
Spirit of God, guiding us back
to revel in Your Loving Presence.
We want to worship You, Source of Sheer Joy,
praising You with all kinds of instruments.

"What's our problem?" we ask each other:
"Why the doldrums?"
We will zero in on You, God, and come
back to celebration, Liberator.

～ 44

In the Old Stories of Your People's roots
all the Glory is Yours, Loving Parent.
You uprooted ruthless idolaters,
cleansed the land, planted families in good soil;
Your Mother Love, not swords, secured their homes.

Wise, Kind Ruler of all: we worship You;
trusting Your Peace Power we pay tribute.

But we sense You have turned away from us,
left us on our own to face scorn and theft;
we are exploited, exiled and enslaved,
treated like the scum, not Salt of the Earth;
renegade movers-and-shakers mock us.

Yet we never forget You and Your Laws;
we bow to You, pleading for Your followers
who are suffering and dying every day.
God, for real You never slumber or sleep?
Are You dozing? Don't You care anymore?

Please come to the aid of our war-torn world:
come soon, Messiah; we trust in Your Love.

～ 45

Our souls expand to praise You, King:
Your Beauty gleams with Light Divine;
Your Generous Words in gold tones ring,
illumined by pure, searing Fire.

We adore You, Ruler Most High,
arrayed in dazzling Majesty.
You surge ahead for Truthful Right;
forging New Paths for humble feet.

You void potentates' prideful claims
with poignant darts of guilt and shame.
Forever You will reign Supreme,
for Justice always guards Your Realm.

Relinquishing our parents' hurts
we bring You gifts from all cultures.
God, form our children as leaders;
give Your Stories fervent readers.

~ 46

God Alive is our Ready Shelter
and first responder in disasters.
Terror can never capture us—
even if oceans cover islands
or an asteroid hits our planet.

Gentle Inner Fountains always flow,
refreshing God's Holy City Home—
this Inviolable Sanctum—
permeated by Spirit Breezes.

Governments battle, finally implode;
demagogues shrivel, hearing God's Word.
God Alive engages and protects us.
Witness God's actions! Wars concluded,
bombs defused, gun metal recycled.
Wait. Watch in awe. Listen. Recognize God
with us and for us here now.

~ 47

Give God a standing ovation
all people of every nation;
voice your joyous adoration.

God's Majesty strikes all with awe.
Peace Prince deals cruelty its death blow,
severs torture's mad, grasping claw.

God names us responsible heirs,
family friends, dear sons and daughters.
We raise praise with royal fanfare.

Open all the stops; cheer and sing!
Call all people to greet Earth's King.

~ 48

God, the Grandest Living Being,
towers gorgeous like a mountain,
drawing all to joyous worship.

God's Good City rises Glorious;
those who threaten her are frightened,
gripped by powerful, gut-wrenching pains.

We sing of the Lion Lamb King,
glimpsing visions of Supreme Peace,
magnificent and always safe.

We worship You, O God of Love:
throughout the world Your fame is sung;
Your honor shines in acts that bless.

God's Mountain shimmers. Common folks
hail Messiah's Wisdom Pillars,
marvel at Great Spirit's Turrets.

Tell your grandchildren God is here,
always leading and guiding us.

∼ 49

Hello, everyone on Earth,
hear Wisdom's Message:
We need not fear clamp-downs;
we can face anyone.

Bank-rolling braggarts cast
fine-spun, deceptive nets,
but freedom is priceless.
Know this, wise guys and fools:
life cannot be purchased.

Every body decays:
animals and humans—
famous or not—all die;
none are self-sufficient;
death takes all away.

Yet we rest in God's Hands.
From death's cell we will rise,
Transformed, Re-created,
to Endless Life with God.

~ 50

Holy God, Highest Good Power,
fills sky from dawn to sunset,
summons all to rapt attention.
Huge and dazzling, God approaches—
no more distant, vague or silent.
Lightning bolts sizzle; ocean tides
surge with the Voice of God the Judge:

Earth and Heaven, be My Jury;
Universe, proclaim My Justice.

All who pledged to serve Me:
come and listen, hear your Sovereign.
No more sacrifice heroics;
I don't need your festive offerings.
Every creature is My playmate,
every birdsong lifts My praises.
Does mother tell child 'I'm hungry'?
Can creature nourish Creator?
Only give Me heart-born Thank Yous;
keep your promises every day;
call Me when you're stressed or
hurting.
I will lead you; you will praise Me.

But, imposters, you stand arraigned—
you who glibly spout My precepts
while at heart despising Scripture.
Those who lust and steal enthrall you;
soon you're lying, hurting dear ones.
When I overlooked your vices
you remade Me to your liking.
Now I summon you for judgment:
Review your God-bereft lifestyles;
sober up and face your sentence.

Humble, grateful people Rejoice;
those who honor Me find Freedom.

~ 51

Ever-loving God
I plead for mercy:
in Your Renowned Grace
expunge all our sins.

Gross guilt always haunts us,
for it's You we have wronged.
Your Judgment is perfect;
justly You sentence us.

I've run amuck all my life
against the steady current
of Your Wholly Wise Spirit,
muddying Your Pure Waters.

Only You can clean up my act.
Obliterate all evil thoughts;
open my soul to Divine Joy;
don't look back at my sad missteps.

Form us as Your New People.
Reform us with Solid Trust
that You'll never reject us.
Grace us again, Live Spirit

with Light that shows other
wrongdoers Your Good Path.
Pardoner, clear my record;
untie my Praise-God Tongue.

No more vain rituals.
Wounded and sorry,
we know You Welcome us.
Restore the Family.

∾ 52

Hey, superstar!
Why broadcast badness?
God sees the shame
beneath your mask,
hears your cunning schemes.
You embrace evil,
love deceiving.

You know? God will humble you for good;
you will be homeless and lifeless.
God lovers will be in awe, but
some will say with a nervous snicker:
"That's the cash-god, people-crushing guy."

We can all thrive like organic trees
in God's Orchard, nourished by Pure Love.
People-Grower, hooray for You always;
Your Wise Acts publicize Excellence.

～ 53

Fools' foul deeds negate God Alive;
all their thoughts and acts are tainted.
God peers into each human heart,
finds none who realize their true need:
all wander; none do any good.
Phonies, don't you know anything?
You're parasites on God's People
with no Spirit Vitality.
On a whim you will wilt in dread;
God's glare reduces you to dust.
Chief Judge, come soon to set things right;
we'll dance in Your Holy City.

∽ 54

God, rescue us for Your Namesake;
power-wash the smears from our names.
Hear us pray; listen, Loving One:
pride and cruelty crush Your People;
godless critics slam good teachers.
Brilliant Spirit, Mighty Ally:
Your Infusion keeps us Vibrant;
You will silence spiteful speakers.
Gladly we'll join to praise You,
humble, generous Vindicator.

~ 55

God, please listen; O God, respond—
we're crazy with anxiety.
Foul-mouthed menaces stampede us:
we're petrified, long to fly far,
escape violence, find repose.

Spirit, frustrate hustlers, mobsters—
always destroying the city—
lying, fighting, hateful, lethal.
God, shock scoundrels with sudden doom.

Dawn, noon and dusk we call on You,
Dear Listening One Who knows each voice.
You draw us from battles unscathed,
Eternal, Unswayable God.
Shear those who flout You down to size;
shorten sultry malicious lives.

We can withstand opposition
and even ignore terrorists,
but can't bear your insults, brother:
we're friends; we worship together.

When believers betray sisters
or slash covenant bonds with gossip
we bring You our bitter dismay
God, counting on Your Healing Love.

～ 56

God, we need encouragement:
proud foes run us down all day long.
Scared, we still trust and praise You.
How can frail humans damage us?
They misquote us, trip us up.
Please don't let evil flourish, God:
get angry; topple empires.
We know You take note of our woes;
You preserve each tear we shed.
We pray, and sense You are with us
as predators run away.
God, we praise You, trust Your Promise.
Your Spirit calms all our fears:
how can mere humans injure us?
Pledged to You, we worship You.
Radiant One, we owe You our lives,
lives drawn from gloom to Glory.

～ 57

Love us, O God:
we throw ourselves
into Your Arms
till these storms pass.

Praying, waiting, we trust Your
Good Purposes, Vision Master.
Your Spirit frees us and shames
pursuers with Constant Love.

Roaring beasts surround us,
hate-speakers, backbiters.
God beyond galaxies:
over Earth shine Glorious.

They tried to trap us,
almost brought us down,
but snagged their own limbs.
Wake up our spirits

with songs before sunrise.
Creator, we will
celebrate You everywhere
with all people groups—

for Your Constant Love soars
beyond imagining.
God beyond galaxies:
over Earth shine Glorious.

~ 58

Leaders, can we trust your speeches?
In your judgments where is justice?
Unjust motives lead to violence.

Envy poisons kids, warps adults;
lies infect all interactions;
psychic powers don't diffuse toxins.

God, please break the spells that bind us:
purge the air of noxious vapors;
clear the land of cruel cynics.

Let Joyful Kindness ever flourish;
all will laud You, God of Justice.

59

Rescue Your besieged people, Great One:
shield and save innocent children from
bloody conspirators ganging up.

Rise and see: will You come to help us?
Rise and chastise, Holy Majesty.
Hear those yapping, sneering curs: will You
laugh them off, Omnipotent Master?

Heart eyes focused on You, we follow.
In every triumph keep us humble,
unmoved by hateful lies and curses.
May people everywhere worship You.

No scrapping fear-mongers can ever
squelch our morning hymns to You,
Triple-Layered Divine Protector,
Invincible, People-Loving God.

～ 60

God, You have gone from us in anger—
but please may we be with You again?
You split the ground: caves yawned; rocks shuddered.
God, heal the land; heal us and all people.
We saw this life void of hope—
in despair's drunken stupor—
but You kept us seeking and lit us
an inextinguishable beacon.

Heaven help us now:
rescue Your loving ones!

"Yes" God announces:
"Israel is Mine; Palestine is Mine.
Lebanon is My Crown,
Jerusalem My Scepter;
I wash My Hands in Europe;
I Stand Tall in Africa,
Rise Brilliant over Asia."

But, now, where are You, God?
Who will show us the way
to Justice, Peace, Safety?
Empower our struggle;
human efforts all fail.

Yet Your Unseen Powers
will quell every rivalry.

∼ 61

God, hear our tears:

From Afghanistan to Zimbabwe
we cry to You with dying breaths.

Bring us to Your High Solid Ground
where we can't go on our own.

God of All Love, our Daily Haven:
we want to be at Home with You always.

You heard our commitments;
You adopted us as Your Heirs.

Peace-Bringer, rule everywhere!
Keep all leaders loyal and loving.

In Your Holy Spirit may we celebrate
and serve You every day.

~ 62

Only God quiets us
in the free space of Peace;
God alone holds our minds
steady in Boundless Hope.

But when will hard knocks end?
We're tired, weak and old,
beat up and broken down,
deceived by sugary talk.

Find quiet with God, dear friends:
God is the Fountain of Hope;
God keeps us in free spaces,
safe and strong in Holy Peace.

Trust God always, everyone;
confide in Creator.
The poor gasp for breath; the rich
fake great life. Both are zero.

Don't rely on stocks and bonds
or let wealth go to your head.
Listen: God is All-Powerful;
God's Love never stops, and God
rewards work well done.

～ 63

O God, You are the One I worship.
We're desperately searching for You,
parched with thirst for Your Living Water.
Once, twice I glimpsed Your Glorious Vigor.
Your Life-Generating Love impels
our self-abandoned, full body praise.
Awake at night I reflect on You,
see You always coming to our aid.
We stay close, hold on, sing poems to You;
Your Holy Spirit fortifies us.
All that would harm or pillage our lives
fades away; You will silence liars,
and God-loving friends will dance with joy.

~ 64

God, hear our cries for help:
shield our lives from panic;
guard against plots and darts,
brash words that wound children.
God, probe those proud, vicious,
booby-trap setting hearts.
Yes, their own base ruses
will bring them to ruin.
"Awesome!" people will shout.
"Oh, yes, God is in charge!
Cheers! Relief! All praise to God!"

～ 65

Hushed in awe we await You,
then erupt in adoration.

All people will pray to You
for You are the One Who responds.

When sins drenched us in chaos
You forgave and purged our guilt.

Your welcome guests know purest Joy,
reveling in Creation's grandeur.

Your acts astound us, God Who gives
Hope to all people everywhere.

You Orchestrate mountain vistas;
You Quiet oceans and nations.

All marvel at Your Splendors;
day and night skies invoke praise songs.

You Tend the Earth, send needed rain,
growing food in lush abundance.

Hills, grass, flowers, trees, animals—
all sound hilarious hoorays.

～ 66

Celebrate God, everybody!
Laugh, cry, sing, dance, play!
Shiver with awe as God's actions
birth faith in fearful agnostics.
All earthlings will worship You, God:
all will give You honor and praise.

Look back. See God's deeds for people:
deep waters split, paths opened; hear
newly freed slaves sing their gladness.
Supreme, Eternal Governor,
You observe cultures and countries;
none can spurn Your Authority.

Praise the Creator, everyone:
loud cheers for God our Life-Saver,
Caregiver, Trainer and Trail-Guide.
You brought us from pit to plateau;
we gather now to give You thanks
as we promised when in despair.

We give You our time and talents
to show and tell all worshipers:
God listens! God hears every song,
moaned or trumpeted; God sees hearts.
God listens, never ignores us.
All praise to You, All-Loving God!

～ 67

God of All Kindness, beam on us;
lighten us up till everyone sees
Your Freeing and Generous Ways.

Holy Lover, may all people
everywhere celebrate You.

Bring countless glad smiles to faces,
songs to voices in every nation,
for Your Justice governs all.

Loving Creator, may all people
everywhere celebrate You.

By Your Lavish Life Force
Earth's produce overflows.

God, please keep beaming on us all
and may everyone revere You.

～ 68

God, You're on the move, dispersing Your foes
like smoke or melted wax facing Your Fire.
But Your followers will revel in Joy,
glad to be with You. Sing and celebrate
Cloud Commanding God, Holy Magistrate
Who adopts orphans and defends widows,
guides lonely people to loving families,
prisoners to freedom while haters burn out.

God, You led Your people through the desert;
mountains shuddered; clouds burst in awe of You.
Law-Giver, People-Builder, Provider:
You fed and revived Your tired, poor ones.
In each generation Your Law of Love
echoes, embodied by faithful servants.
Warlords and bombers dash away from You
God, as You rest with us and Bless each home.

Your Sheltering Wings dazzle like sun on ice;
Your Glorious Reign Outshines all dynasties;
Your Kingdom shall outlast every mountain.
Your Entourage gleams with millions of stars;
thousands of angels circle Your Dais.
As You ascend, those You enthralled follow;
many, even old enemies, bring gifts.

Praise the Kind One Who each day lifts our loads,
cuts down the headstrong and extricates us
from death's talons. Watch glad celebrants
rise and assemble. Herald singers lead;
girls with tambourines dance with marching band.
Mass choirs led by children sing joyous praise;
in colorful clothes all the lands' leaders come.

God, display Your perfect power again:
kings' and queens' gifts will adorn Peace City;
God, humble bully nations, disperse those
who thrive on war; may they pay You tribute.
Give God praise with native songs, all nations;
praise God Who rides intergalactic skies,
Whose Voice thunders, Whose Strong Love ever shines.

Wondrous, Transcendent One, You overrule all,
empowering humble ones. We worship You.

~ 69

God, rescue us: Your Ark is sinking,
mired in muck with no solid footing;
inundated with requests for help
we're beyond our depth, flooded with tears,
sick of crying, tired of praying.
We're hated; we're punished unjustly.
You see our stupid sins, gross failures;
Spirit, may our faults not deter seekers.
Those who hate You take it out on us;
we're scorned for mourning, teased for fasting.
Source of Life and Love, we call to You:
Come near and answer; free us from doubts;
draw us from this morass, this abyss.

Don't let demons engulf faith families;
see how proud ones revile and shun us?
No one cares when their jibes maim us,
souring minds, embittering souls.
May their lavish meals make them sick,
lurid visions induce blindness,
greed keep their backs always bent.
Scatter them from homes and cities;
pummel them always with their guilt;
may they fade away, forgotten.

But revive Your oppressed people.
We will overflow with praise songs
in grateful, passionate worship;
humble peacemakers will smile.
Be encouraged, you who seek God:
God listens to needy people,
cares about addicts and inmates.
Skies, islands, oceans, creatures
all give the Earth-Renewer praise.
God will restore communities
where our children will be at home.

∼ 70

O God, rush to save the children!
Hurry to help each hurting one.
Drive abusers crazy with guilt;
shame slave-drivers to stop and weep.

Assemble all who yearn for You
in glad festive worship. O God,
Your children are in desperate need:
Please hurry, come here. Help! Don't wait!

~ 71

We are safe with You, God;
Keep us confident in Your Goodness.
Hear us pray; save us, even from ourselves.
Shelter us always sane in Your Spirit.
Come retrieve us
from the clutches of those up to no good.
We have looked up to You,
trusted You from youth;
You blessed our mothers with healthy childbirth.
We will always thank You.
Praise percolates through us all day long.
Please do not leave us:
we are old, neglected, cheated.
Stay close, Lifeguard. Help, now! Come right away;
shame our accusers.

Bright with Hope we will praise You more each day.
God, inspire us till we tell our children
all the Good You do.
Your Love radiates endless as the sky—
who compares to You?
Though You test us with many bitter tastes
You will revive our flagging spirits
gently, tenderly.
On pianos we'll praise Your Fidelity
and tell Your Grace in poems, Wondrous God.
Indoors or out we will sing You loud hymns—
happy and carefree in Your Company.

~ 72

God, guide Earth's leaders to restore
justice for all oppressed people.

May all lands be free and fertile,
meeting the needs of each poor child.

We long for that promised New Earth
ruled forever by Messiah
where Peacemakers will always thrive.

Your Reign embraces the Cosmos;
distant princes will bring You gifts;
all will be honored to serve You.

Poor, weak folks are Your First Concern:
You will prevent or avenge their deaths.
You will bless all, and all will praise You.

Come, Promised One, ever Alive,
ever receiving prayers and praise.

Dance for joy, verdant hills and fields.
Come, shine forever, Creator!

Cosmic Miracle-Working Being:
come fill all Earth with Your Brilliance.

∼ 73

Surely God treats good people well—
but how old envy shakes our faith!
Rascals flaunt nonchalant violence.
Their minds are stupefied with greed,
their tongues putrid with taunts and threats.
Yet folks feast on their vacuous boasts—
while rogues sneer "What does God know?"
and pile up wealth with no worries.

What good are our humble, clean lives?
Every day we face new hardships.
Whining smudges our witness and
we are perplexed, frustrated—till
we sit still in Your Holy Place.
There we can see rich fools dancing
down slippery slopes to ruin,
panic, abrupt death. All gone soon—
forgotten when we wake with You.

Old envy was sapping our joy—
we were deaf, dumb and blind to You.
Still You are always with us, God,
guiding by Your Pure Love Spirit
till we go Home Sweet Home for good.
What or who but You could we want?
Though our minds and bodies weaken
You always bless us with Courage.
We love living with You, Peace Prince—
broadcasting Your Love-Driven Acts.

∼ 74

God-Man, why are You gone
for what seems like forever?
Are You frustrated with us?
You died for us, remember?

You lived with us on Green Earth.
Come now to her ravaged hills;
see how cut-throats abuse her,
chop down trees and bloody fields.

God, the ground is scorched and stripped,
most signs of Your Glory gone;
no sounds come from prophets' lips.
When will destruction be done?

Why restrain Your Power, God?
You rule oceans and seasons:
come Revive the Earth You made;
remember Your suffering friends.

Listen, look at the violence.
Creator, You have the Clout:
may poor folks praise You again:
don't let mockers drown us out.

～ 75

God, You are famous here and now;
we love talking of Your Great Acts.
You convene Heaven's Council when
Earth, nations and people totter.
You command boasters "Be quiet!"
Musclemen: "No more hits or threats."

None can hoist themselves to honor.
You weigh hearts—humbling, exalting:
You pour forth Judgment like spiced wine;
each evil mind must drink its fill.
We will keep on praising You, God;
You put down wrong and lift up Truth.

～ 76

Faithful strugglers tell Your praise, God.
You live in Holy Peace City
where all weapons are recycled.

You are more lofty than mountains,
undimmed in Luminosity,
unquestioned in Authority.

Your Voice dismantles war machines;
no power invokes awe like You.
Who can bear Your anger's Passion?

Earth waits hushed for Heaven's Verdict:
Emancipation for All.
Even angry young men respect God.

Moved to make and keep promises
we pledge ourselves in service to God
Who humbles violent rulers.

~ 77

"God, help! God, hear me!" I cry,
drowning in discouragement,
inconsolable, sleepless.

I searched for You, God,
ached for Your presence.
You kept me awake,

filled with wordless ponderings,
recalling visions of You,
poems composed in nights long gone.

"Are You done with us, God?" we wonder;
"Will You never look our way again?
Where is Your Famous Love?"

We review Your Miracles,
marvel at the Holy Strength
that freed and formed Your People.

Chaos shrank from You;
Fire, Wind, Water, Earth
heard and revered You.

Your People could not see You,
yet Your Servants escorted
them tenderly through each storm.

～ 78

Listen, dear people, to story-talking
from our grandparents—to us, to our grands—
of God's Good Power shown in Wondrous Actions.

God's Law set our ancestors on Right Paths:
they taught their children who in turn taught theirs;
but some turned away, discounted the signs.

God parted waters, ordered seas to stand,
led them in cloud by day and fire at night;
God cracked desert rock, made water stream forth.

Yet distrustful, they whined for bread, then meat,
filled their bellies on the plenty God gave,
but stayed bound to cravings, gripped by fears.

Their prayers were empty efforts to appease,
lip service negated by faithless deeds
which God Who is Mercy always Forgave.

Freed slaves forgot God's plagues on their masters,
the ways God directed, the land God gave;
but God never forgot those wayward ones.

Only idolaters roused divine ire;
for years God let them suffer and die.
But gathered, still gathers the faithful remnant,
guided by true, Servant-hearted Shepherds.

∼ 79

God, the community You created
has been devastated and degraded:
toxins, deserts, landmines strangle the Earth.
God, when will the shameful disasters end?
Will poor people be ravaged forever?
God, punish shameless polluters instead;
don't let us suffer for grandparents' wrongs.
God, we're hurting; open Your Heart to us
with Your world-famous, Gracious Forgiveness.
No more "Where's God?" jeers! Unveil Your Justice,
hear prisoners' cries, revoke death sentences;
make God-mockers drunk on their own spiked brew.

Your Loyal Family will praise You always
with new passion in each generation.

∼ 80

Hero of all people, King of Angels:
grant us an audience.

Look with favor on El Salvador;
come in Your Brilliance
to Mexico and Guatemala.

Mobilize Your Powers;
come rescue destitute people.

Renew us, Master,
in Your Loving Vitality.

All-Powerful One,
how long will You glower at us?

Our meals are drowned in tears;
people laugh at us, deride our efforts.

Renew us, Master,
in Your Loving Vitality.

As displaced peoples, freed slaves and refugees
You cared for us tenderly,

blessed us abundantly,
enabling us to bless others.

Why now do You neglect us?
Look our way; come soon, Messiah.

Help us live in Graceful Harmony,
centered in Your Powerful Peace.

Energize us, Holy Spirit;
we want to be faithful in prayer.

Renew us, Master,
in Your Loving Vitality.

～ 81

Sing out your gladness to God
Who Loves and Empowers us.
Tune your instruments;
strike up the band!
Let the celebration begin,
a day of praise and thanksgiving
honoring our Liberator.

God's Spirit speaks to quiet hearts:
"I broke your shackles,
shouldered your load;
you cried and I responded,
brought you through storms,
tried you in times of drought.
Listen now, you need to listen:
don't worship toy gods;
I am God Who formed and freed you.
Open your souls to Me;
I'll fill you with Love, Joy, Peace.
For years you refused to listen;
I let you go it alone.
If only you would hear Me now
and learn my Way of Peace—
how soon I'd turn foes to friends,
God haters to awed worshippers.
You would all have your fill
of whole grain bread and pure honey."

～ 82

God the Supreme Judge
tries all Earth's judges,
probes their unjust judgments
for they favor evildoers.

God commands: "You shall be Advocates
for homeless, jobless, helpless people.
Come to their defense; maintain their rights;
bring their oppressors to justice.
You so-called judges are foolish,
blind to flagrant injustice
which ruins people and planet.
You swore in My Name to uphold Justice:
I gave you this Divine Task,
though you are only human,
soon gone and forgotten."

Holy Supreme Judge
of all nations and rulers:
come render Judgment on Earth.

～ 83

Please don't sit there like You can't hear us;
don't stand still doing nothing
while Your opponents posture and snarl.
They're out to stigmatize people of faith,
conniving against Your followers,
conspiring to divide us, until
Your Worldwide Community dies
and no one knows Your Name.
Terrorists rise and dictators thrive;
the gods of war and wealth dominate.

Rout them, O God, as You have before:
sweep off those who pillage the Earth;
chase them with tornados and hurricanes.
May they die in shame—
yet finally appeal to Your Mercy—
realizing Your Supremacy.

～ 84

How exquisite Your Home, Strong God!
We are homesick for Your Garden,
thirsty for Your Life-Spurting Presence.
We envy song sparrows
who nest in green canopies
feeding their fledglings.
O God, Majestic Creator:
how Happy to be Home with You
voicing Your praise all day!
How Joyous, drawing Purpose and Strength
for Adventurous Pilgrimage with You.
Your Spirit turns bitter tears to Healing
Streams, desert valleys to Rain-Garden Ponds.
Your children grow livelier, each year
nearer to seeing You in Person.
Hear us pray, Strong God;
see our faces wet with tears and sweat.
Better a day at Home with You
than a thousand nights on the town.
We would rather wash windows in Your House
than dine at a five-star restaurant.
God, You're our Sunlight and Shade,
always beaming, always giving,
never holding back blessings
from Salt-of-the-Earth People.
Joy-Filled are all who rely on You!

～ 85

God, You looked with Love on lands
where conscientious ones labored
giving them Peace and Plenty.

You forgave their offenses,
cleared the record, forgot Your fury.
Look on us now, Pure Love.

Long ago You spent Your anger,
bore the brunt of it Yourself.
Why can't we realize You are All Love?
Will Your Spirit renew our joy?
Gladly we hear Your Peace Promises;
may we not fall for foolish bluster.

Your Way frees us in awe of Your
Brilliant Love alive here, now.
When Your Passion awakens our faith
Justice marries Peace, and
Truth is Born on Earth.

You will supply our needs
from this Earth You gave us.
Organic farmers lay the groundwork.

~ 86

Hear us, Master, respond to us:
we're overwhelmed with needs.
Keep Your Loyal Servants
Viable and Vibrant.

God of Love, the One we Trust;
in Mercy hear our all-day requests.
We turn to You, hopeful, expectant,
counting on Your Generous Forgiveness.

You pour out Love on all who call:
God, in Kindness hear our tears.
We pray to You whenever we're needy,
knowing how You listen and reply.

No so-called god is like You, O God—
Creator, History-Maker.
People of every ethnicity
will kneel in Your Presence.

All will celebrate Your Majesty—
One, Only, Miracle-Working God.
Show us how to live Your Good
Tried-and-True Loving Way.

Wake us to full attention
in total awe of You, Master,
dancing Your Love always,
for You lifted us from doom's dump.

Proud antagonists keep needling us.
They completely ignore You,
Ever Serene, Patient God
Who overflows with Undying Love.

View us with Your Mercy Eyes;
invigorate our service,
Humble, Noble Master—
as You did for all our ancestors.

Display Your Great Goodness,
quieting all naysayers.
God, You are our Life Support,
always giving Strength and Solace.

~ 87

God builds New Peace City
on Golgotha's High, Holy Ground
where blood-drenched Love reached far beyond Israel.

God's Home-Place outshines all Earth's Wonders.
From all nations New Births are Certified—
Egyptians, Arabs, Russians, Chinese—
while choirs and bands spurt praise fountains.

∼ 88

God! Lifeguard! Higher Power!
People cry to You 24-7.
Please come: God, listen,
hear the demon-plagued, the living dead.
We call to You for inmates of hellholes:
beaten down, isolated, left to die,
relentlessly punished,
loathed by former friends,
trapped, jailed, silenced, blinded.
God, we keep on crying, praying for them.
Are they better off dead?
Must we die before Your Miracles start?
No, we plead with You anew each morning.
Why are You ignoring Your People?
Look how children are neglected, abused!
We are all terrorized, drowned in disasters.
God, You are leaving us alone in the dark!

～ 89

We will never stop trying to voice
Your Divine, Ever-Living Love,
embodied in humble people.
Countless galaxies sing of You
in tune with heaven's angel choirs.
Holy Mystery of the Universe,
how can we ever describe You?

All Powerful, Ever Loving,
You outshine all bodies of light,
surpass all heavenly beings.
Commander of Ocean Surges,
You quell storms and armies alike.
Author of the Laws of Nature,
mountains sing Your Strength and Beauty.

You move us to True Compassion
illumined by Your Wise Judgments.
How blissful to let loose in praise,
our lives a dance in Your Love-Light.
Proud to wear Your Royal Colors
we acclaim You, Spirit Guardian.

Your Love came Full Strength in Peace Prince,
Pledge of the end to war's chaos.
In His Name we call You Parent,
follow Him into Your Throne Room.

But we are unruly children,
disgracing ourselves and Your Name;
we lose Your Protection and Aid.
When will You return, Holy Love?
How long staying angry, aloof?
Our human lives are brief, You know.
What's the goal? Only doom and death?
Where's Your Promised Unending Love?
Silence mockers, Most Worthy One;
keep us sounding Your accolades.

∼ 90

God, You were always our Spirit Home.
Before the births of mountains and planets,
before all beginnings, beyond all ends—
You were, You are, You will ever be—God.

Our millennia are mere days to You
while families grow, divide and die away.
Fear of Your disproval scorches us;
You gaze on the oozing scabs of our guilt.

Each day of our seventy, eighty-some years
brings some torment, leaves some grief—and flees.
If only we knew Your rage is not blind—
our paralysis would turn to awe.

Move us to take stock, making each day count,
forgiven and free to forgive others.
Show us Your Love as we wake up each day;
Joy will fill our years, Glad Days exceed sad.

Teach us who serve You Your Way of Working;
may our children see Your Wondrous Power.
May we sense Your Delight in us, Parent,
Your Seal of Approval on what we do.

～ 91

At Home in Your Sheltering Presence,
we stay in Peace—hidden, protected,
for You are our Living Sanctuary,
Strong Holy One—right here with us,
guarding us against pitfalls and pests.

Like a mother bird with her nestlings
You always have us covered.
Your True Love is our bullet-proof vest;
we are free of all fears, immune to
hypochondria and paranoia.

Though thousands rush headlong to death,
their obsessions will never seduce us.
All who claim You as Safe Haven
will be at Home in divine Shalom,
never dislodged or endangered.

You assign angels to watch over us;
they carry us over sinkholes,
past obstacles and would-be attackers.
Guardian, You keep us Free and Safe
as our hearts hold fast to You in Love.

While we call we sense Your Ready Response.
You are with us on downsides, in tight spots,
saying: "I will bring You to my High Ground;
your life will be long and satisfying,
filled with vistas of My Liberation."

~ 92

We are delighted giving You thanks, God—
telling Your Love in poems at dawn or dusk
while friends play sweet praise on keyboard and strings.

We are ecstatic about Your Actions,
overjoyed with all Your Works-in-Progress,
dumbfounded at the depth of Your Reasoning.

Wrong grows fast; perpetrators are blind
to their certain and permanent doom.
Your foes vanish; Your Honor is Supreme.

Spirit, You Empower and Endow us.
You will frustrate every opponent
while godly people flourish like palm trees.

Towering like strong, august sequoias,
rooted in Your Garden Home, we still thrive
wherever transplanted on the planet.

Our verdant fruit-bearing years never end:
"God is Good all the time" we testify;
"Great Spirit, our Holy Mountain Fortress."

～ 93

Love King rules in Cosmic Splendor,
arrayed in Holy Energy.
Nature's course is fixed and stable.
God, You have always been In Charge,
Creating and Re-creating.

Restless swells surge and billow;
madness threatens to drown You out.
But Your Vigor always prevails;
Your Voice is Irresistible,
Your Home ever Pure and Lovely.

~ 94

God of Justice, beam Your Searing Judgment;
pierce evildoers' proud facades.
When, God? When will they stop gloating?
They stifle Your children,
treat widows, orphans, refugees like dirt,
sneering "Who cares? Who even sees?"

Oh, knuckleheads! When will you get a clue?
How can the Original Seer not see?
The Quintessential Ear not hear?
Why would the Supreme Judge of all nations
not hold violators accountable?
Do you think the Divine Teacher is dumb?
God perceives every foolish scheme.

What Joy to be Your student, Master!
Your Book is our Life-Spring
in media wastelands,
Your Altars our Oases
while con-artists fly by.
You will never neglect Your Dear Ones;
judges will again judge justly,
every honest heart concurring.

"Who comes to our defense?" call boy soldiers.
"Who pleads our cases?" cry raped girls.
Without God we would be voiceless and dead
but we whimper as we fall
and Love responds, lifting our spirits,
gradually, tenderly
replacing our fears with Strong Joy.

No way can corrupt governments
whose laws demean humanity
claim divine association.
Thugs join forces to hurt good souls
but God is a Wall of Protection.
Hard blows bounce back harder
on those who inflict them.

God's Searing Light still judges,
pierces, incriminates.

~ 95

Come join the Joy Song
shouting hooray for Holy Spirit!
Join the parade to give God thanks,
a musical extravaganza
to honor Peace Prince.

God is the Grand One
over all angelic beings.
God rules deep in Earth's core
as in highest mountain formation;
oceans and islands all answer to God.

We come to worship our Creator,
bowing, kneeling, together,
silently, sheepishly,
before our Holy Shepherd.
We come to listen:

"Be soft-hearted" God says.
"Open your hearts and minds to Me;
don't be bull-headed like your ancestors
who resisted My guidance
and never found a time or place to rest."

～ 96

Everyone on Earth, sing New Songs!
With Creation itself voice God's praise!

Every day sing the Glorious Ways
Creator Revives all kinds of people.

God is worthy of Supreme Honor,
more awesome than any
so-called divinity.

Those local deities are idols.
God birthed light and cosmos
with Life-Generating Power.

Come to worship God, all tribes and tongues:
gaze on God's Majesty;
honor God with your gifts.

Be awestruck by God's Holy Beauty.
God established the Laws of Nature
and justly judges every human.

Smile, wide skies! Dance, cloud puffs!
Echo praises, oceans!
Sing for joy, fields and trees!

Let the whole universe celebrate
Creator's return to Creation.
At last—truth, peace and justice for all!

~ 97

Love Personified rules Earth—
Bright Hope for every island and beach!
Veiled by manmade clouds God's Justice governs.

Lightning bolts hint at God's Boundless Power.
Earth shivers; mountains erupt and shrink
before the Holy Sovereign.

Galaxies sing out God's Glorious Goodness.
All who flaunted idols sink in shame
and fall down to worship the Creator.

Relieved, we welcome Your Wise Rulings.
Master, You are Infinitely Greater
than any human-devised deity.

God-Lovers shun violence.
The Holy Spirit shields precious children,
keeping tender hearts free of evil.

God's Life-Light grows as good souls
gladly follow Love's Brilliant Ways.
We dance for Joy in sync with Peace Prince,
acclaiming Holy Majesty.

~ 98

Sing the old song with a new tune
for God's Astonishing Actions.
Sing of Life-and-Death Freedom won
with Holy Power for all to see.

Sing the fame of Promises Kept
through countless generations; sing
of God's Earnest Kindness, Constant,
Sacrificial, Outrageous Love.

Pull out all the stops now—Loud Joy!
Outbursts of song in all cities:
piano, horns, drums, guitar, voices
pour out Joy in God's Grand Presence!

Oceans reverberate: Earth and
all its inhabitants rejoice;
rivers applaud; hills join in praise.
All-Wise Monarch will Rule Justly.

~ 99

God is Sovereign:
be shaken, heads of state.
God presides, flanked by angels:
shiver, Planet Earth.

God is Supreme,
beyond time-space dimensions—
Awe-Inspiring in Every Culture—
Holy Creator.

God's Royal Strength
shines in Passionate Justice,
treating each person and nation fairly.
We worship You, Great Spirit.

Ancient seers yearned to speak with You, God;
You responded to their prayers.
They obeyed Your Laws, heard Your Voice;
You gave them fresh starts
after self-concocted botches.

We worship You, Holy Spirit,
Expeditor, Wise Director.

~ 100

Let loose a cascade of Joy
resounding worldwide!
Sing, laugh, shout! Enjoy God
in worship and work.
God created us. We are
Love's precious children.
Come eagerly with your gifts
and heart-song tributes.
God is always Good: Love's True
Kindness never ends.

~ 101

Our hearts sing: O God, You are Love!
We praise Your Wise Justice.
Are we on the Right Path?
How we long to see You!
We want to please You every day—
Heart Eyes Pure, Focused, Kind.
We want to steer clear of deceit,
gossip and snobbery.
Praying and moving with those who
care for Your Creation,
day by day we work to banish
violence from the land.

∼ 102

God, let us know You Hear us crying now:
some gasp for breath in smoke-filled rooms or huts;
some are crazed with fever, too sick to eat.

Congolese mothers mix tears with ashes
to feed stick-boned children, while lone voices
cry like hoot owls on poles, mourning lost trees.

God, how can we rest in this violent world?
We're damned if we do and dead if we don't.
What are we to You—a moment's trifle?

God, You are world-famous throughout history:
the one they called Good Shepherd proved You Care;
Isn't it time to Intervene again?

Forgive our nostalgia for dead churches:
some day all cultures will grace Your Kin-dom;
We trust You Listen to poor people's prayers.

God, You shrank to live in our dimension;
You Hear moans from death row and hospice beds.
Move us to write twenty-first century psalms.

May Your Truth soon magnetize all people
Ever-living God, let no more youths die;
at last may our children know and serve You.

~ 103

Pour out praise, Dear Sisters—
Extreme, Inside-Out Love.
Recall all God's Giving and Forgiving;
Freeing our bodies from diseases;
Liberating our psyches from demons.
God treats us Royally, Tenderly,
Fulfilling our Purest Desires;
we are Ever Young, never weary.

God's Justice Releases oppressed people;
through Moses God Revealed the Law
and through Israel how to keep it.
Divine anger is rare and soon gone;
God is not out to punish us
even when we deserve it.

Divine Love is deeper than outer space,
wider than the measureless cosmos.
God Feels our pain like a Mother,
Knows us better than our mothers
and Understands our short lifespan viewpoint.

God's Love Opens doors to Eternity,
Forges Paths of Peace and Justice
for our children, for people all over.
Love Governs: pour out praise, angels;
display Love's Splendor, Creation.
Pour out praise to God, Dear Brothers.

∼ 104

Honest Friends, keep pouring out praise.
Your Highness, robed in blinding light:
You draw back the curtain of deep space;
clouds escort You; winds form Your pathways;
gusts and flames are Your couriers.

You founded Earth; You keep us grounded;
You set oceans' bounds, supply abundant
fresh water for all Earth's creatures;
Your streams nourish all that is green.
You provide the perfect habitat
for each creature from treetop to cavern.
You choreograph Celestial Cycles;
we with all creatures follow Your Rhythms.
Who can count Your Live Inventions?
Who can fathom Your Wise Actions?
We traverse the oceans You filled with life;
Your pet whales play in the waves.
All life depends on You for food:
hold Your Breath or look away and we die;
Your Spirit Revitalizes.

Everlasting, Majestic Creator,
Earth-Shaker: revel in Your Creation.
Honest souls, always sing psalm poems to God.
(Master, we pray You enjoy our writings
as we delight in composing them.
Let self-absorbed writers not publish.)
Praise God altogether, Honest Friends.

∼ 105

God, we purpose to honor You
and publicize Your Work worldwide.
Spirit, we treasure Your Presence,
inquire of You, rely on You.
Keep us earnest in pondering
Your Astounding Actions and Words.

You solemnly promised in Love
to lead Your People safely Home.
You protected nomads, migrants;
kept kings from killing Your Prophets.
Before the great famine You sent
Joseph to Egypt, brought him through
slavery and jail to high honor.

You gave the Hebrews large families;
they were resented, mistreated;
You raised up Moses and Aaron,
affirmed their words with deadly signs;
the slaves walked out, Liberated.
You stayed with them in cloud and fire,
put up with all their murmuring,
nourished them with manna and quail,
split desert rock; Fresh Water Flowed.

You kept (still keep) Your Promises,
leading people Joyfully Home
to Live Right, caring for New Lands.
Yay, Peace Champion, we praise You!

~ 106

Allelu the Holy Spirit:
praise God's Goodness, Limitless Love!
What poet can paint Creator's works?
What words are worthy of Peace Prince?
God, help us live in Your Family—
Free, Just, Joyful, honoring You.

Like the Hebrews we're ungrateful;
often we doubt Your Wise Power
and discount Miracle Rescues.
Yes, after the Red Sea crossing
they sang ecstatic praise to You,
but soon reverted to whining.
You disciplined them; their souls shrank,
bodies sickened, lives were snuffed out.
If Moses had not intervened
You would have turned away for good.
(Even Moses lost his temper.)
O God, those You brought to New Land
killed children on idol altars,
debased themselves, tainted the ground.
You let foes defeat and rule them,
yet could never hold back Your Love
and You softened their captors' hearts.

God, draw us now from all nations,
Free and Joyful, worshiping You.
Allelu Unnamable One:
You were, are, and always will be.

~ 107

Give God thanks for Divine Goodness and Infinite Love. People from all continents, speak up; prisoners whose bonds were broken, record your stories.

Lonely souls—restless, parched, dispirited, barely alive—cried "God? Help!" And God freed them, guided them to roots, to Hometown. Thank God for Endless Love in Amazing Goodness to people—meeting needs, assuaging yearnings.

Souls blinded and bound by their own disdain of God's Way struggled and toiled alone; finally cried "God? Help!" And God freed them, guided them to Holy Spirit Truth. Give thanks for God's Boundless Love in Amazing Goodness to people— breaking shackles, opening jail doors wide.

People insane with fear and hate, addicts deathly ill—too sick to eat—feebly cried "God? Help?" And God freed them, guided them with Holy, Healing, Reviving Words. Give thanks for God's Infinite Love in Amazing Goodness to people. Speak up, joyful, grateful people; sing out your stories!

Souls at sea, crossing vast oceans saw celestial panoramas. Lifted on fifty-foot swells, then plummeting; groping for footholds, handholds, they cried "God! Help!" And God quieted the tempest, guided them to shore. Thank God for Endless Love in Amazing Goodness to people.

Praise God in church circle and town square. God owns all streams, all soil and air. Cities where injustice is rampant will shrivel to desolation. But God will Empower poor people to Transform deserts to lush fields surrounding vibrant cities where large families will Flourish. God-Lovers observe and sing for Joy while the arrogant are ignored, ousted, evildoers silenced.

Treasure the Stories, sages; reflect on God's Boundless Love in Action.

～ 108

We are ready with You, God—steady and ready,
up before dawn writing new lyrics for familiar tunes,
yearning to sing Your Worth to all the world.
Your True Love is sky high, vast as the cosmos.
God beyond galaxies, over Earth shine Glorious;
come to the aid of precious humans.

Your Spirit speaks to our hearts;
You give us this Good Earth.
Every nation must answer to You,
must conserve Your Green Canopy.
You rule in Peace forever.
who will show us the way to Your Royal City?

God, have You abandoned us?
Manmade peace is an illusion.
You alone will purge us of greed
unstrap us from war's madness.

∽ 109

God, the One our words praise,
please speak up for us now.
Hateful lies, baseless gibes
hurt loving, praying folk.

God, expose the meanness
of those who malign us;
it is You they oppose.
Let their fake prayers backfire.
End their greed-based careers;
topple their dynasties.
Shorten lives of tycoons
who exploit slum-dwellers.
May the curses rogues spew
permeate their psyches.

Good Loving God, help Your
hurting, heartbroken followers.
We're fading fast, ignored,
despised, feeble, hungry.
Help! Show Your Famous Love!
Shame the persecutors.

We want to give You praise
in mass congregations
and in twos or threes, for
You stand strong with the poor.

～ 110

God said to Messiah:
"Sit here on my throne;
rule the Universe in Peace;
all will honor You."

God's Majestic Word
transforms foes to friends.
Armies of Eager Volunteers
radiate the Gospel of Peace.

God commissioned Peace Prince
as permanent High Priest.

By Divine Justice
tyrants are deposed,
every death-dealer destroyed.

God-Lovers imbibe Pure Living Water
and Shine with Vigor.

~ 111

Allelu God!
Pairs, trios, crowds love giving voice to praise.

God's Creation
stirs Joyful Attention, Boundless Wonder.

All God's Actions
radiate Royal Eternal Perfection.

God openly
displays Extravagant Spirit Love.

God nourishes
each worshiper and keeps every Promise.

God's Power works
Peace and Justice for lands ravaged by war.

God rules always
in Absolute Truth, Unswerving Goodness.

God rescues us,
pledges undying, Re-creating Love.

Wisdom begins
with respect for God; those who live God's Way

grow in Understanding,
raising allelus all ways, forever.

~ 112

Joy comes in Holy Awe to those
who Love Living by God's Rules.
Their descendants are Vibrant
Earth-keepers in Happy Homes.

Some will become wealthy, but
will remain uncorrupted.
In bleakest hours New Hope shines
for God's Kind, Grace-Filled People.

Happy are the Generous
who work to maintain Justice.
Nothing disrupts them; they will
leave a Lasting Legacy.

No threat distracts from God's Love;
they are bold and fearless,
knowing Peace will prevail.

Their Endowments Empower
poor Youths to earn high honors.
Envious minds sulk and die.

∼ 113

Allelu God!

Loving Servants raise God's praise—
praise to the Holy Spirit
here and now and forever.

From Beijing to Berlin,
from Conakry to Chicago,
everywhere Messiah reigns—
suffused in Heavenly Light
yet focused on Planet Earth.

God brings outcasts in, welcomes
vagabonds as Honored Guests.
God blesses lonely people
with joyful homes and families.

Allelu God!

∽ 114

Peace Prince leads people to New Exodus—
from mute bondage to Music-filled Free Space.
Chaos demons vanish in God's Presence;
Earth shivers in awe; Creation dances.
Spirit summons Fresh Water from bare rocks.

~ 115

God, we are not seeking glory
for ourselves or our nation.
But for Your Unending Love—
Your Extreme Love—that silences
world-wise, now-where's-God jibes.

Holy God, Alive in Glory,
You move and act as You desire.
Manmade gods are voiceless, senseless,
blind, deaf and mute like their makers.

Attention, people: trust the One
Who always keeps us Strong and Safe.
God knows us; Holy Spirit Joy fills all
true worshipers—young, old, rich, poor.

God cares for us and our families.
God Who Made and Owns the Cosmos
Entrusts Earth to Human Stewards,
Blesses us with Gifts for Service.
Allelu God!

～ 116

We love You for hearing our tears.
                              You always listen:
we bring You our fears, needs, desires and dreams.
When we're sick to death, frustrated, grieved

we wail for healing: "God, help! I give up!"
                              You pour forth love;
You shield simple people and restore hope.
Stay at peace, troubled souls: know God's blessing.

You brought us from death's haunting slide
                              to new Spirit Life.
Though lies and hurts mount, You keep our trust strong.
How can we give thanks for all You have done?

Here's to You, Master, source of true freedom:
we pledge You our lives, day by day offerings.
                              You weep for our deaths.
We worship You, God. Hail Resurrector!

∾ 117

Allelu in every language!
All people, praise God
Whose Immense Love never ends.
Hail the Highest One!

～ 118

Give God thanks: Divine Love Thrives forever.
Tell it, prophets: God's Patient Love never fades.
Echo it, priests: Peace Prince Loves, no matter what.
Be awed, people: God Loves everyone always.

Tied in knots we cried "God, help!" You freed us.
You're always right here with us: we have no fear;
who can hurt us with Your Spirit shielding us?
We are secure, safe with You, not depending on manpower.

Warped doctrines besieged our minds;
in the Liberator's Name we blanked them out.
Gurus sounded calls; in the Holy Name we tuned them out.
Worry drove us to the brink, yet God was there with Joy Power.

Happy voices commemorate Holy Spirit's Great Works.
Be gone now, death; we live to tell our stories.
God disciplined but never abandoned us.
Blessing doors open; thank God Who Listens, Who sets us Free.

Suffering Servant—despised, tortured, dead—arose alive,
revealed God's Essence of Life.
Re-creation has begun: we celebrate!

Set all people free, Master. Bless our work;
bless all Your Servants. We praise You, Creator,
worshipping in Festive Joy. Your Holy Peace Shines on us.
Thank You, God! Your Love persists forever.

～ 119

Happy People live by Your Standards, God—
always listening, looking for Signs from You,
gladly, naturally doing what's Right.
O God, we want to be guided by You,
to You; no more missteps, thank You Spirit.

How can our lives be pure and vigorous?
By direct Holy Scripture Infusions.
God, by Your Goodness we live to serve You:
help us grasp Your Amazing Ideas;
we're lost in this world of money and war.

We're desperate to see Your Promise Fulfilled,
our lives renewed by chewing on Your Word.
Remove the pall of blindness and falsehood
that dilutes our delight in Your Teachings.
We long to serve You Who Freed us to Love.

Shepherd, teach us to live like You, always
joyfully perceiving Your Good Purpose.
Focus our spirits in Your Peaceful Way,
free of all trifling or greedy pursuits.
Come, Holy Spirit: You are our Lifeline!

God, we Love to feel the force of Your Words.
Before, we ignored You but now we listen,
trusting Your Chastening, growing in Wisdom.
Although know-it-alls say we don't know You,
Your Precious Word Treasures gleam from our hearts.

God Who made us, come off the page to us.
Your Rules ring true, though we learned the hard way;
hold us up; keep us Vibrant by Your Love.
Beyond smokescreens Your Goal keeps us on track.
When will proud, lying bullies be derailed?

Your Book is timeless, True as the Cosmos,
compelling as Nature's Laws and Rhythms.
Without Your Voice we would die in despair:
Life-Guide, how Your Message Liberates us!
Humans are limited; You're Infinite.

We always Love musing on Your Good News.
God, Your wisdom takes us beyond violence
to ageless, intrinsic, Brilliant Vision.
Your Teachings taste better than any treat;
Your Prudent Counsel outshines all beacons.

No more vague god-talk. Let us face Your Truth,
not fight wrong with wrong—be Strong in Your Peace.
God, we are in awe of Your Rule of Law;
free us to abide by Your Peace Treaty;
draw us near, away from war's greedy reach.

Spirit, keep us living, learning, Loving.
Whatever You say is forever True.
God, we follow You Who know our motives.
Rejuvenate us to praise You, Savior;
may we hear anew Your Claim on our lives.

～ 120

From under big guns
we cry to You, God,
trusting Your answer.
Free us from false friends'
syrupy delusions.
Spirit, when will You
pierce dull consciences?
Why are we here in
these warring nations
waiting forever
for Shalom when bomb
stockpiles keep rising?

∼ 121

Gazing into skies above mountains
we wonder "Where is our Life Support?"
All from You, Cosmos-Generating,
always alert God. You sustain us:
in active Spirit You are right here
keeping us Sane and Safe, protected
from every harm; You watch over all
our entrances and exits always.

～ 122

All week our Eager Joy was building:
now to worship! Let's go! We're ready!

Together in Your Holy Presence
we can picture Your City of Peace,

built for vibrant unified worship—
all tribes and tongues as One Family,

celebrating, thanking, praising God,
Maestro, Composer, the Word Alive.

We pray for Peace in every household,
Peace and Quiet in every city.

For Your sake, Master, we'll work for Peace.

~ 123

God, we look to You
in Your Unseen Realm
like children who sense
Mother's every move.
We need You to look at us
with Sympathy and Kindness:
clear off the scorn tossed on us
for all these years, Father Love.

～ 124

If You had ignored us,
if Peace Prince had not come
when rage was eating us—
we would have been devoured.
You Liberated us,
broke death-and-terror's lock,
Creator Redeemer!

~ 125

God, trusting You fully,
our spirits are soaring.

We live in Peace City
surrounded forever
by Your Towering Presence.

Violence is over,
vicious cycles have ceased.

Let Your Goodness blossom
in kind-hearted people.

God-Man, bring lasting Peace
to flower everywhere.

~ 126

Master, sometimes Your coming here
to live with us seems like a dream.
We smile seeing You dawn on new
faces in all nations, praising You
Who died and rose. We praise You,
Love King, and pray please return soon.
Like rain to parched ground may our tears
waken long dormant seeds of Joy.

∼ 127

Only God's Love makes houses homes;
God alone can protect our towns.
Why overwork early and late?
God Loves giving us rest and sleep.
Children are God's Choicest Blessing,
keeping us Vigorous and Bold.

~ 128

Lost in awe of God—gladly
following Peace Prince—what Joy!
We delight in the rewards
of Spirit-Energized work.
Our marriages and children
Flourish like fruitful orchards.

Humbly we give You all praise,
Giver of all that is Good.
May we live to see Your Truth
embraced by our grandchildren.

～ 129

For as long as we can remember
we have cried for poor oppressed people.
Loving God, long before we were born
Your Dear Ones were being beaten down,
plowed under, yet never defeated,
for You, Good God, Revive and Set Free.
Now we pray, pour shame on peace-haters;
may they shrivel like grass in gravel.
No harvest for hatred, not even
"Hello, God bless You" from passersby.

～ 130

From this hellhole our souls yell:
Help! O God, please hear; please care.

God, if You listed our misdeeds
who could measure up?

No, You forgive all, even as
God-People forgive torturers.

Messiah, when will we see You?
We're waiting, watching for some sign.

All our hopes are pinned on You:
Redeemer, come free us soon.

⁓ 131

God, we don't want to be self-righteous,
don't want to look down on anyone;
no ivory towers or success ladders.
We want to be humble and quiet,
serene as children on mother's lap.

Wait, dear God-Lovers, filled up with Hope—
watch and wait now: Messiah's coming.

～ 132

Holy One:
As Pilgrims on Your Servant Way
we recall Faithful Sojourners—
who worshipped You, trusted Your Promises,
though sometimes they lacked food, rest, or shelter.
Promised One, born in Bethlehem:
many heard You in Jerusalem.
Today in all towns we gather—
listening, singing "Master, come soon."
Keep Trail Leaders true to Your Map;
guide us always, as You Promised.
Loving One, be at home with us;
feed the hungry; radiate Peace.

~ 133

Imagine the ideal:
God's Family living together in Love!
Eye to eye Healing Tears flow;
heart to heart new blood surges;
mingled lives Flourish
always in Divine Favor.

~ 134

With Spirit High Priest
all day we serve God;
all night raise God's praise.
Together on Earth
in Heaven's Dimension
we praise You, Creator God.

∾ 135

Allelu God in work and worship:
God is all Good, gives all Joy.

God, Who is Supreme over all kings,
yet chooses to live with poor people.
God's Will is Law throughout the Cosmos,
summoning clouds, rain, lightning, and winds.
God dispatches the angel of death,
dispenses with nations' demagogues.
People will always worship You, God;
You champion the cause of human rights.
Manmade gods cannot do anything;
idol worshippers become idle.

Faith Community, allelu God;
friends of Peace Prince, praise the Awesome One
with angels in New Shalom City.

～ 136

God of all Good Gifts, thank You:
>Your Love never ends.
God over all kings, thank You:
>Your Love never ends.

Sole Power beyond nature:
>Your Love never ends.
Source of Creative Wisdom
revealed in sky, sea and land,
beamed from stars, planets, and moons:
>Your Love never ends.

You Freed us, broke slavery's bonds;
through grave dangers You led us:
>Your Love never ends.
You deposed evil rulers,
Blessed lowly people with land:
>Your Love never ends.

You will meet everyone's needs.
Thank You! Thank You for Live Hope!
>Your Love never ends.

～ 137

All around the world
songs are dying; people are crying
with longing for Peace.

Money and guns demand Freedom Songs.
God, how can we sing
when all power mocks Your Harmony?

Yet we can't forget
glimpses of Your Holy Peace City.

Without that vision
hands go limp, voices are stilled, Joy dies.

God-Man? Peace Prince? Please
stop child-killing, spiraling violence.

∼ 138

Holy Loving One:

We want to go all out in loving You.
(Angels, gurus, guides: hear us praise God Supreme!)
All will tell and sing praise, indoors and out,
for Your All-Embracing Love never stops.

In Word made human You outdid Yourself.
Holy Spirit, You Embolden our prayers.

We long for every king to sing Your praise;
may leaders listen to You, Glorious One,
for You come and care for the lowest ones
but always keep Your distance from the proud.

Master, You Revive and Empower us
in the vortex of suffering. Your Spirit
diffuses anger, Frees us from hatred.

We trust Your Perfect Justice and Mercy,
Holy Creator, Ever-Loving One.

∼ 139

You have probed me, Loving Spirit;
You see me from every side. You
Understand where I'm coming from,
every impulse, each intention.
You know when and where I will go.

You Embrace and Cover us, God:
we're overwhelmed by Your Presence,
Holy Love Breath. No matter where
we fly, no matter how we feel,
You always Guide and Steady us;
day and night Your Light is constant.

Gentle Spirit, You form all souls;
before birth You shape each person.
We praise You, Awesome Creator!
You preview each day of our lives—
God, how Boundless is Your Wise Love!

Your Endless Visions entrance me:
I wake up sensing You right here.
How we wish You'd wipe out evil!
Keep bloodsuckers away; may we
avoid those who vilify You.
All who oppose You, we oppose.

Probe my motives, Loving Spirit;
see my fears: am I off Your Path?
Keep me on Life-Without-End Way.

～ 140

O God, please free us from evil's
clutches; deflect blows brutal people
inflict from mean schemes in daily battles.

Make us immune to their toxic words,
biting voices and violent acts;
keep us on track when proud rogues set traps,
designing webs that distract and confuse us.

Generous God, Messiah of Promise:
listen, look, help! Have compassion on us,
Powerful Liberator, King of Peace.

Frustrate greedy tyrants, God; foil their plots;
feed bullies the fruit of their own vile threats;
strike them with lightning; let floods swallow them.
Chase away liars, haters and brawlers.

We rest assured You stand up for the poor;
honest souls praise You, thrive in Your Shalom.

~ 141

O God, my spirit calls out to You:
Do You hear me? Please let me know!

Receive each deep breathing prayer;
accept all body-soul prayers.

Spirit Guide, monitor my speech;
seal my lips when I should not speak.

Keep me free of anger's allure,
that lush seedbed of hurtful deeds.

May I accept correction;
thank You for wise discipline.

Thicken our prayers to ward off evil;
let ruthless rulers fall.

Shepherd, we are Focused on You,
Peaceful with You; please stay with us.

May we avoid booby traps
and trappers themselves fall in.

$\sim$ 142

Wounded ones yell for attention,
pleading to see Your Compassion
for parents' tears, for children's screams.

Our spirits collapse, but You, God,
see us past camouflaged pitfalls.

No one but You notices our plight;
we have no safe place, no lifeline.

Still we call "God, You are our Safe Place!"
You Provide all we need for Life.

Hear the crescendo of despair
from diseased and displaced people.

Set Free every soul and body
to sing together "God is good!"

~ 143

Listen, God; hear our tears:
we rely on Your Kindness.
Call us Your Servants
but please don't judge us;
no human can meet Your Standards.

Gloom pursues us, chokes our spirits.
We think about those ancient times
when You worked Many Miracles.
Arms up in prayer we reach for You,
thirsting for Your Loving Spirit.

Come soon, Master: hope is shrinking;
without You we are scared to death.
Yet we trust You all through the night:
show us Your Love in the morning;
we trust You to Guide us all day.

Free us from fear and greed, Spirit:
we're Home Safe and Happy with You.
Move us to please You, Holy One:
Revive us by Your Word;
Free us from confusion.

Gently Calm our conflicts,
turning foes to friends.
We want to serve You, God.

~ 144

Allelu God! You are rock solid
yet gentle as breath; cool as water
yet fierce as flame. Teach us to Wage Peace.

God of True Love, Wall of Protection,
Liberator and Sanctuary:
You Empower us for leadership.

God, we marvel that You Care for us—
human beings with such dim, quick lives!
Yet we hear You broke heaven open.

Come back soon, Holy Light: expose all lies;
burn away arrogant deception;
Free us from bitterness and chaos.

Our new poem songs will feature Your praise,
for You raise up true Servant Leaders,
preventing every self-serving ploy.

All children will Thrive like healthy trees;
there will be plenty of food world-wide;
no invasions, no more refugees.

Joyful Peace grows with You, Loving King.

～ 145

We proclaim Your fame, Master;
always we will raise Your praise.
Who can fathom Your Greatness?

Parents tell sons and daughters;
grandparents rave of Your Actions.
We are speechless in Wonder!

God, we sing and celebrate
Your Patient, Extravagant
Love for each of Your creatures.

All creation beams Your praise;
Loving people honor You,
Glorious Promise-Keeper.

You raise up lowdown people.
All creatures rely on You,
Provider of food for Life.

Vast, Timeless God, You come close
to those who open their souls
in frank prayer and rapt worship.

～ 146

Allelu God! Praise God all souls!
Yes, we will always give God thanks,
glowing with lifelong heart-song Joy.

Human rulers cannot free us:
they die; their foolish schemes fizzle,
but Your gifts Enliven our Hope.

You Conceived, You Generate all
matter and life. Without reserve
to the Nth Degree You Love us.

You stand up for oppressed people;
you Bless those who feed the hungry
and Guide prisoners to Freedom.

Life-Light, You Open blinded minds;
You Lift up lowly ones; You Care
for lonely and helpless outcasts.

God Loves those who work for Justice
and thwarts those who act unjustly.
God Rules always; allelu God!

～ 147

Hooray, yay, God! What Joy to give You praise!
We play with words to voice strong thanks;
our tributes sound from piano keys.

You Build up Faith Communities,
Bringing back wandering children,
Healing wounded and broken hearts.
Master, You Promote the humble,
but the arrogant hit bottom.

You count and name each of the stars—
Your Strength and Wisdom are Boundless!
You unfurl clouds full of raindrops
that grow grains for creatures to eat.
You Speak: frost forms, snow drifts, hail falls—
who can face frigid wind-chill temps?
You Speak again: melting begins—
balmy breezes and gurgling streams.

Machines and brawn don't impress You,
but You Treasure those who respect
Your Awesome Strength and Energy.

Peace City, rise, salute the King
Who nourishes and protects us.
Scripture Lovers, Word-Enfleshed Followers
Receive God's Call to Merciful
Justice anew. Allelu God!

∼ 148

All praise to God! We visualize
constant praise in the Unseen Realm—
angels on mountains in mass choirs,
clouds, suns, moons, planets. With one voice
the Universe gives praise to God
Whose Voice created all, Whose Word
Powers nature's unchanging Laws.

Deep ocean creatures give God praise!
Lightning, rain, hail, snowstorms praise too;
gale force winds serve and honor God.
Mountains and plains, all kinds of trees,
all animals radiate praise.

May every person worship God.
Leaders and citizens worldwide—
men, women, children, Young and old—
all will raise praises to Peace Prince,
Glorious, Universal Sovereign
Who Gathers and Empowers us,
permanent Love Kingdom Agents.

~ 149

Allelu God!
Write new Holy-Spirited songs
for diverse God-adoring throngs.
Earth-dwellers, enjoy our Maker;
kind hearts, celebrate the Savior.
Dance for Joy; play piano; beat drums.

God Loves to honor humble ones
who savor Creator's Good Gifts
and resist official violence.
Allelu God!

⁓ 150

Praise our Maker!
From Holy Ground through Vast Cosmos
sound forth praises
for all Life-Generating Acts.
Praise Glorious God
with trumpet fanfare, orchestras,
bands and dancers;
praise with each native instrument.
Sing praise, every living being!